HISTORY OF TRUCKS

Bruce LaFontaine

DOVER PUBLICATIONS, INC.

Mineola, New York

Bruce LaFontaine is an illustrator and writer living in Rochester, New York. He specializes in science and technology, space and aviation, transportation, military technology and natural science. His books include *History of Space Exploration Coloring Book, Bridges of the World Coloring Book, Motorcycles Coloring Book* (all published by Dover Publications) and *Our Solar System* (World of Science/Safari Ltd.). His artwork has appeared in a variety of publications, including *Scientific American, Air Classics, Wings, The Wall Street Journal* and Gannett newspapers. He is a graduate of Rochester Institute of Technology and the State University of New York.

Copyright

Copyright © 1996 by Bruce LaFontaine.
All rights reserved.

Bibliographical Note

History of Trucks is a new work, first published by Dover Publications, Inc., in 1996.

International Standard Book Number

ISBN-13: 978-0-486-29278-6
ISBN-10: 0-486-29278-9

Manufactured in the United States by LSC Communications
29278916   2020
www.doverpublications.com

INTRODUCTION

Trucks first appeared in the United States and Europe during the 1890s. The trucks of this era, however, in terms of design, were little more than automobiles modified to carry light loads. They were propelled by steam and electric as well as gasoline engines, and they featured such now-antiquated equipment as oil- or gas-powered headlights, solid-rubber tires and chain-driven rear wheels.

In the United States, truck manufacturers like Ford, Mack, White, International and Studebaker grew into industry leaders by producing progressively bigger and better trucks. Improvements in roads and the growth of the interstate highway system helped to create a market for larger and more powerful freight-hauling vehicles.

By 1920, the gasoline engine was the power plant of choice for almost all American trucks and cars. It grew in size from the first small four-cylinder model to the in-line six-cylinder engine, and ultimately to the powerful V8. One of the early vehicles that proved most adaptable to truck design was the Ford Model T. It was modified for use as a light pickup truck, a tanker, a flat-bed truck, an ambulance and a panel delivery van. Its successor, the Model A, also proved very adaptable.

During the 1930s and early 1940s, American truck design began to reflect the look of the automobiles of the era. Especially popular was the streamline and curvilinear style that so heavily influenced American industrial design during this period. The truck industry grew rapidly during this period, and production skyrocketed during World War II. By 1948, manufacturers were building more than one million vehicles a year.

Trucks now account for a significant portion of the total motor vehicle market, and their use is no longer confined to commercial operators. During the last ten years, sales of the four-wheel-drive "Sport Utility Vehicle" have reached an all-time high in both American and worldwide markets. Commercial trucks have developed into comfortable, even luxurious, multipurpose vehicles while still retaining their utilitarian function. Because of their versatility, ruggedness and innovative technology, the success story of American trucks is certain to continue into the future.

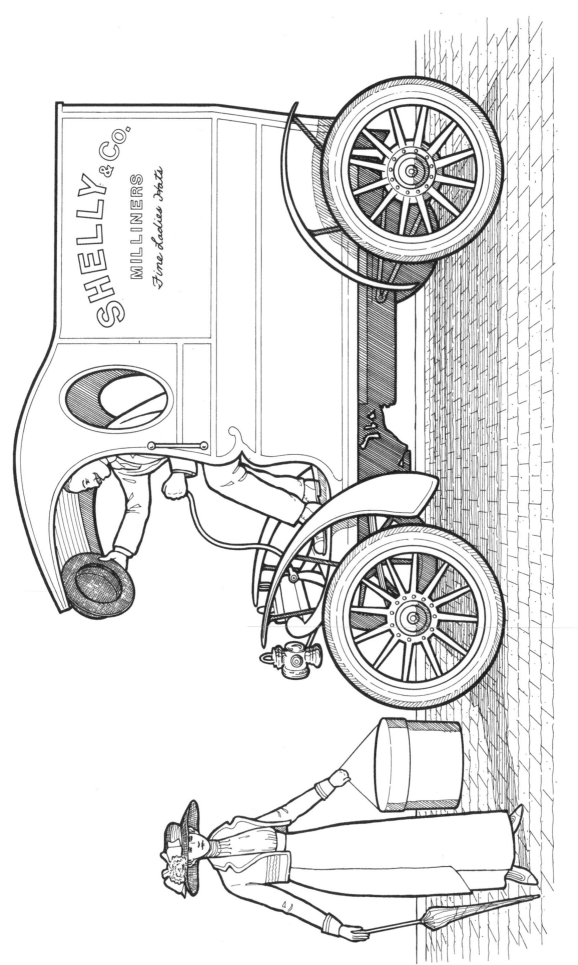

1904 Oldsmobile Light Delivery Car. The Olds Motor Works was founded in 1897 by Eli Ransom Olds. The company became part of General Motors in 1908, but continued to build cars and trucks with the Olds nameplate. The light delivery car was available with either a one-cylinder, 7-hp, or a two-cylinder, 10-hp gasoline engine. It was steered with a tiller, like that of a boat rudder, rather than a steering wheel. It had oil- or gas-powered headlamps and came equipped with the new pneumatic, or air-filled, tires developed by the Goodyear Rubber Company. This Olds was one of only 700 trucks on the road in 1904; by 1918 that number would rise to more than 500,000.

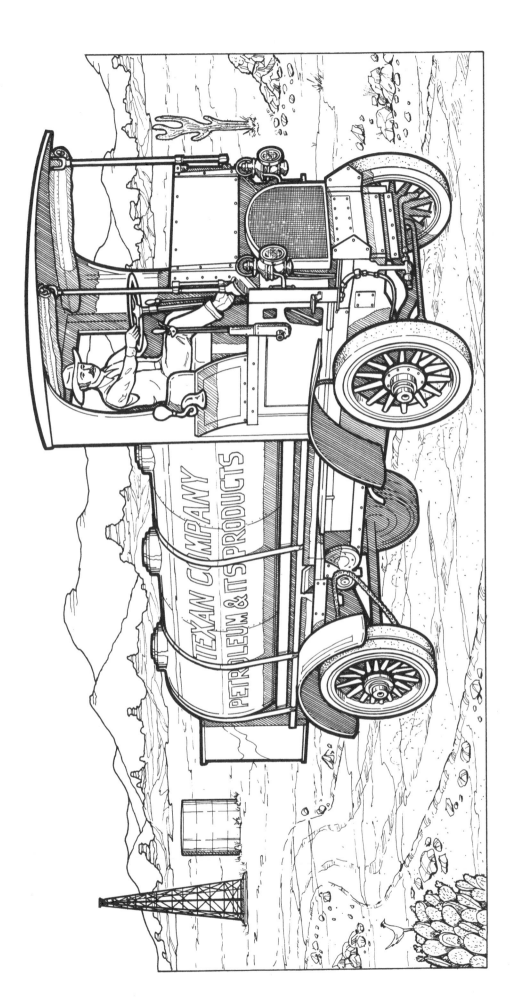

1910 Mack Cab-Over-Engine Four-Ton Tanker. A great name in the history of American trucking appeared in 1902 with the founding of the Mack Truck and Motor Company. By 1911, Mack was manufacturing more than 500 trucks per year and was well on its way to establishing what would become a worldwide reputation. The phrase "built like a Mack truck" has become a common expression to denote strength and solidity. The Four-Ton Tanker shown here had a four-cylinder engine that developed 36 hp and turned the rear axle with a chain drive. The high, open cab was positioned over the engine and had canvas side curtains for weather protection. It used solid-rubber tires wrapped around steel wheel rims.

1911 Seitz Platform Stake Truck. By 1912, there were more than 460 firms manufacturing automobiles and trucks, though most of these companies produced vehicles for only a few years before succumbing to competitive pressure. One of these short-lived truck builders was the Seitz Company, which was active from 1911 to 1913. The stake-bed model shown here was chain-driven by a gasoline engine and was equipped with solid-rubber tires. It had a load-carrying capacity of 1,500 pounds and sold for $1,200.

1913 Ford Model T Closed-Cab Delivery Truck. Henry Ford revolutionized the world of transportation with the mass production of his Model T automobiles and trucks. Ford began truck production in 1905 with their Model C Delivery Van. This 1913 Model T Wood-Bed Delivery Truck had a four-cylinder, 176 cubic inch, gasoline engine producing 22 hp. It was equipped with Goodyear pneumatic tires, and gas- or oil-powered headlamps. Ford's assembly-line production techniques enabled him to build more than 100,000 vehicles in 1913.

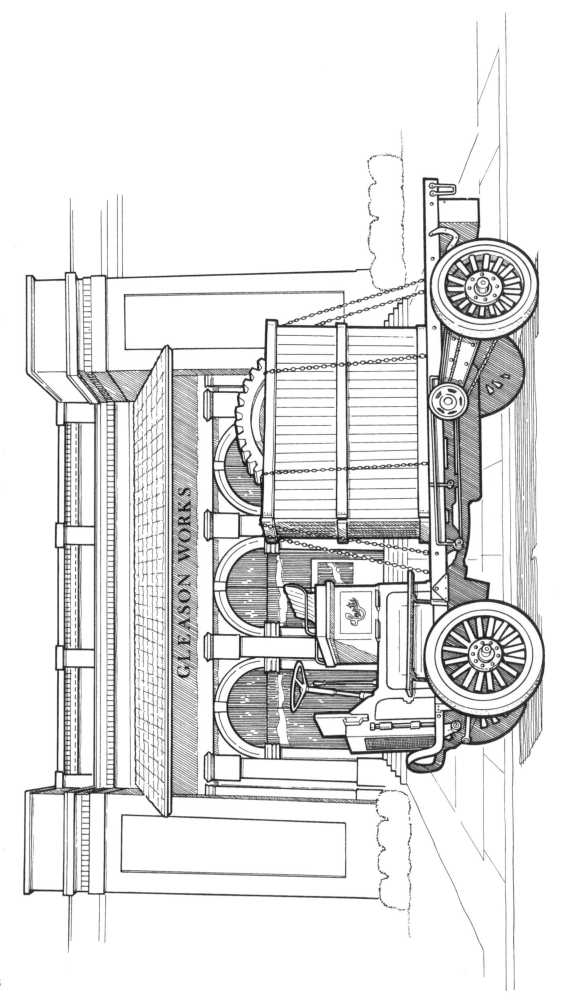

1914 Curtis Flat-Bed Truck. This two-ton flat-bed truck was a product of the Pittsburgh Machine Tool Company of Braddock, Pennsylvania. It was powered by a four-cylinder engine that developed 27 hp and used a chain drive. It sold for around $3,000. It is pictured in front of the Gleason Works of Rochester, New York, a manufacturer of gear mechanisms.

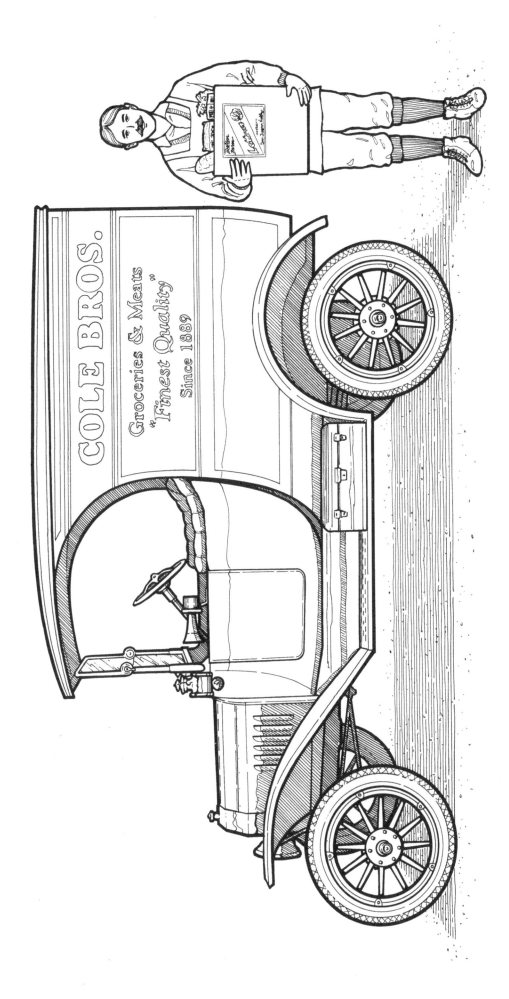

1915 Ford Model T Delivery Van. Another version of the Ford Model T truck was the light-duty delivery van shown here. It used the same rugged and reliable four-cylinder, 22-hp engine as the earlier Model T's, and was equipped with pneumatic tires and electric headlights. By 1922, there were more than one million Model T trucks on America's roads.

1918 Four-Wheel Drive Canopy Express U.S. Army Truck. The needs of the military during World War I caused a dramatic increase in truck production. The U.S. Army purchased more than 100,000 trucks between 1916 and 1918 from dozens of manufacturers, including this vehicle, built by the Four Wheel Drive Auto Company of Clintonville, Wisconsin. With its four-wheel drive, this type of vehicle was ideally suited for transporting troops and supplies across the muddy battle-fields of France and Belgium. After the war, a huge surplus of American trucks remained in Europe, contributing to the popularity of American vehicles in overseas markets in the decades to come.

1920 Mack Model AB Delivery Truck. The Mack delivery truck shown here was powered by a four-cylinder engine that generated 36 hp. It was chain-driven and equipped with solid-rubber tires. The cab could be protected from bad weather by a sliding wooden panel on the lower half of the door and a roll-down canvas side curtain on the upper half. It also featured a hinged windshield that served as a natural air conditioner. The Mack Company would continue to build chain-driven trucks into the early 1940s.

1924 Mack Model AC Flat-Bed Truck. The Model AC was known as the "Bulldog" because of the distinctive shape of its front end and hood. Introduced in 1916, the Mack "Bulldogs" became one of the most recognizable vehicles on the road. This 1924 model was equipped with a four-cylinder, 58-hp engine, had a hand crank for starting and could carry a load of up to three tons.

1925 Dodge 3/4-Ton Panel Commercial Car. Another great name in the history of American trucking appeared in 1914 with the introduction of vehicles built by the Dodge Brothers Motor Car Company. Dodge trucks soon developed a reputation for strength and reliability. By 1926, the company was manufacturing 26,000 trucks per year.

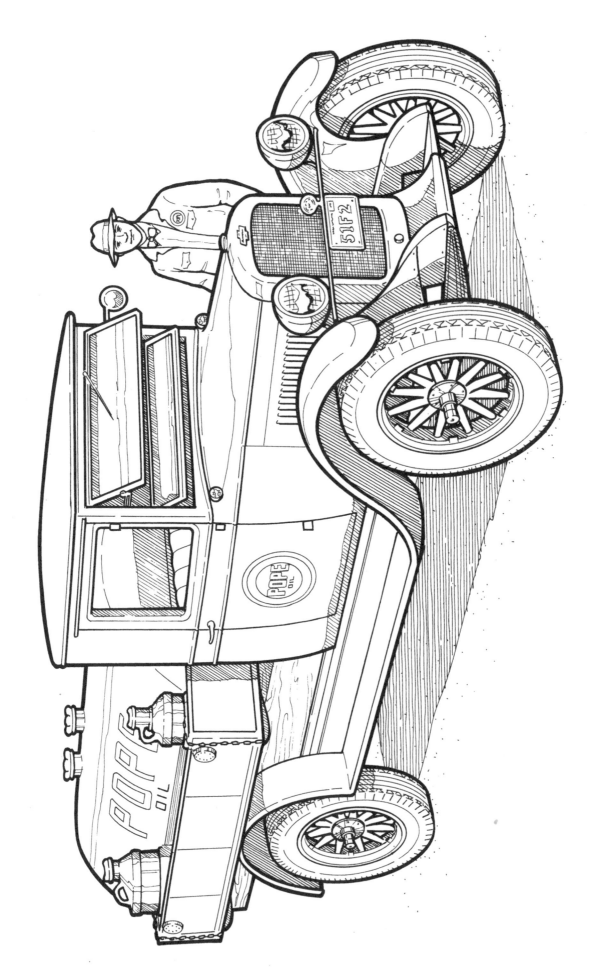

1926 Chevrolet Tanker. From the earliest years of the automotive industry, Chevrolet Motors played a leading role in the construction of light trucks, and they have continued to play that role to the present day.

This Chevy gasoline tanker was equipped with a 35-hp, 170-cubic-inch, four-cylinder engine. It had a double-hinged, divided windshield to aid cab ventilation.

1930 Ford Model A Mail Truck. The Ford Model A, successor to the Model T, was introduced in 1928. It was powered by a four-cylinder, 200-cubic-inch engine that produced 40 hp. Unlike the Model T, which came in black only, the Model A was available in a choice of colors, including blue, green, red, brown and orange. Prices ranged from $385 to $570. So popular was the Model A that by 1929 more than 100,000 had been sold.

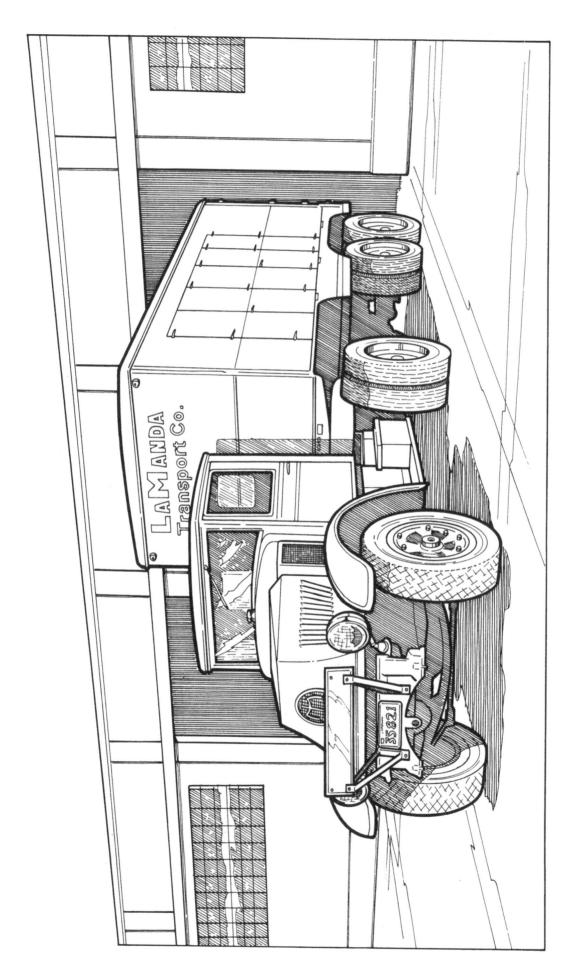

1932 Mack AP Tractor with Fruehauf Semi-Trailer. When it was realized that the engines of trucks could pull greater loads than the trucks themselves could be built to carry, a new type of transport vehicle appeared. It combined a cab unit or "tractor," housing the engine, with a detachable "semi-trailer" that held the cargo. In a way, it was a throw-back to the concept of the horse and wagon. The Fruehauf Company of Detroit became the first firm to specialize in building semi-trailers. This Mack AP "Bulldog" tractor was equipped with a six-cylinder, 290-cubic-inch engine producing 78 hp, and the Fruehauf trailer could carry 15 tons.

1932 GMC Tractor with Sleeper Cab. One of the most successful companies in the truck-building industry is the Truck Division of the General Motors Corporation. This tractor was available with a large, powerful six-cylinder, 11.7-liter engine producing 173 hp. The cab was fully decked out with quadruple air horns, spotlights and a curtained sleeper cab. Sleeper cabs were introduced in the late 1920s and immediately became very popular with long-haul truckers.

1934 Ford V8 Log Truck. Ford trucks were fitted with V8 engines in 1932. With more cylinders and greater power, these trucks were able to pull much greater loads than their four- and six-cylinder cousins. The model shown here was available with either a 136-cubic-inch, 65-hp V8 engine or a 221-cubic-inch, 85-hp V8 engine.

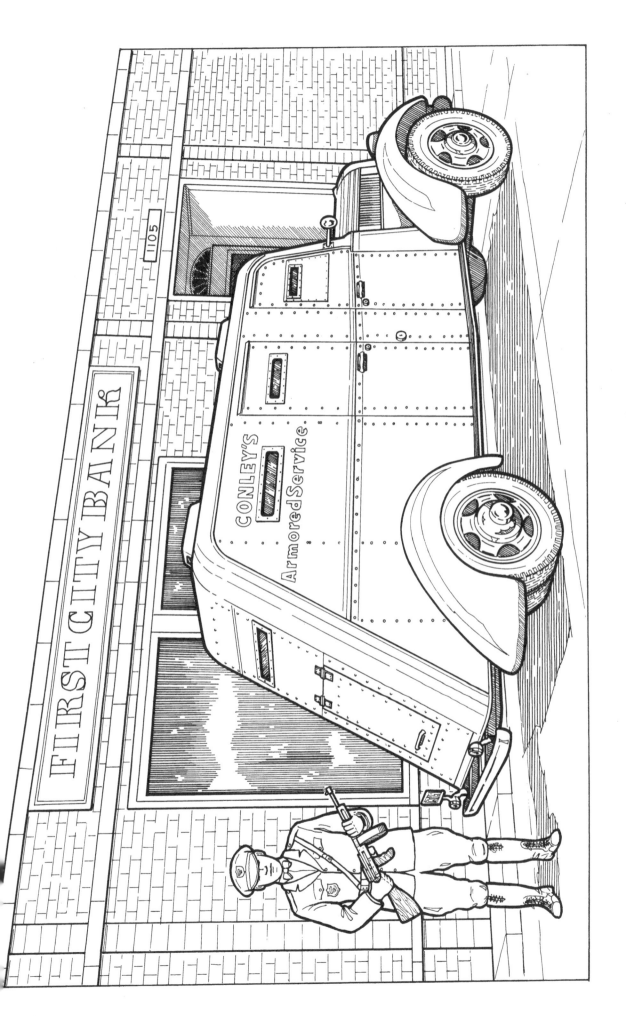

1937 Ford Armored Truck. The beginnings of the new emphasis on streamline design are evident in this Ford armored truck. It incorporated the flowing lines and teardrop-shaped fenders that were characteristic of this body style. The truck's frame, or chassis, and its engine were built by Ford, but the armored metal body was constructed by the National Steel Products Company. The truck could carry a load of one ton.

1938 International Model DS300 Delivery Truck. International Trucks was founded in 1907 and by 1929 it had reached a yearly production level of 50,000 vehicles. This 1938 cab-over-engine model was available with either a four-cylinder, 132-cubic-inch, 37-hp engine or a six-cylinder, 213-cubic-inch, 78-hp engine. In 1938, International Trucks sold more than 76,000 vehicles. The company is still building trucks for the worldwide market under the name Navistar, adopted in 1986.

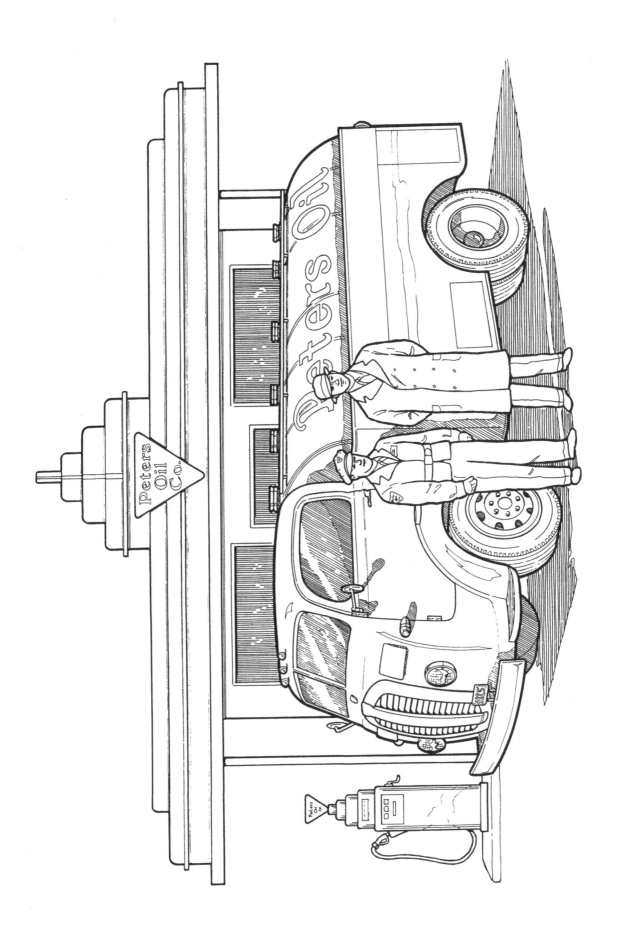

1938 Dodge Six-Compartment Gasoline Tanker. The Dodge Brothers Company was purchased by Chrysler Motors in 1928, but trucks and cars continued to be built under the Dodge nameplate. This tanker truck was powered by a six-cylinder, 218-cubic-inch engine developing 75 hp. Its flowing lines identify it as part of the streamline design style pioneered by Chrysler Motors with its 1936 "Airflow" automobile. Dodge truck production for 1938 totaled more than 53,000 vehicles.

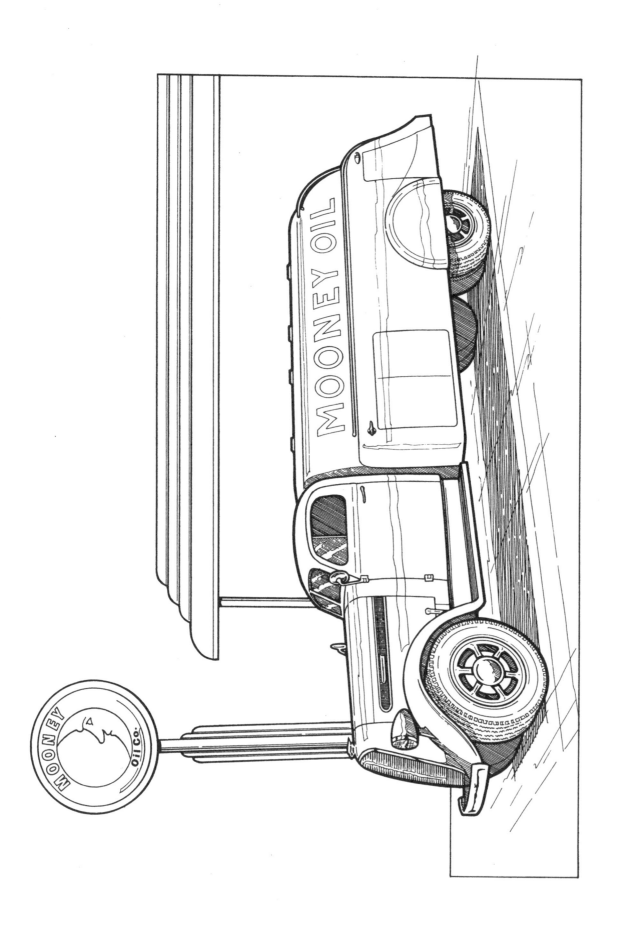

1938 Studebaker K-30 Three-Ton Tanker. Another respected name in the history of American trucking was the Studebaker Motors Company. The company began building electric-powered vehicles in 1902 and gasoline-powered cars in 1904. Gasoline-powered trucks were first manufactured in 1911. This streamlined K-30 gasoline tanker was equipped with a six-cylinder, 226-cubic-inch engine producing 90 hp. The long-nosed styling reflected the preferences of designers of the period, and the rounded fenders, flowing lines, teardrop headlights and skirted rear wheels all show the influence of the movement toward streamlining.

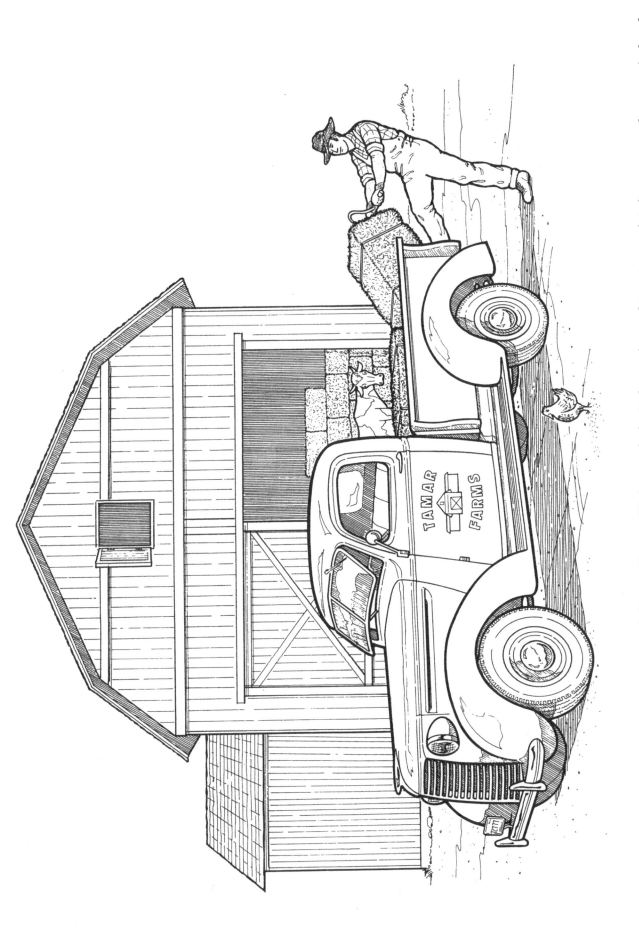

1939 Chevrolet Half-Ton Pickup. A dependable workhorse of light-duty trucks, this 1939 Chevy half-ton pickup was one of more than 169,000 built during that year. Available with a six-cylinder, 216-cubic-inch, 90-hp engine and two-tone paint, it was rugged, economical and stylish, a perfect personal and work vehicle for the American farmer, who became a major purchaser of small trucks after World War I.

1939 International Model D30 1½-Ton Tanker. Not only the truck pictured here, but the gas station to which it is delivering fuel, have been influenced by the design school of streamlining. Vehicles so designed were more aerodynamically efficient, but that wasn't the reason for

building them this way, as evidenced by the appearance of the style in everything from the new glass and steel architecture to home appliances. It was more an attempt to beautify the machine and celebrate the promise of American technology.

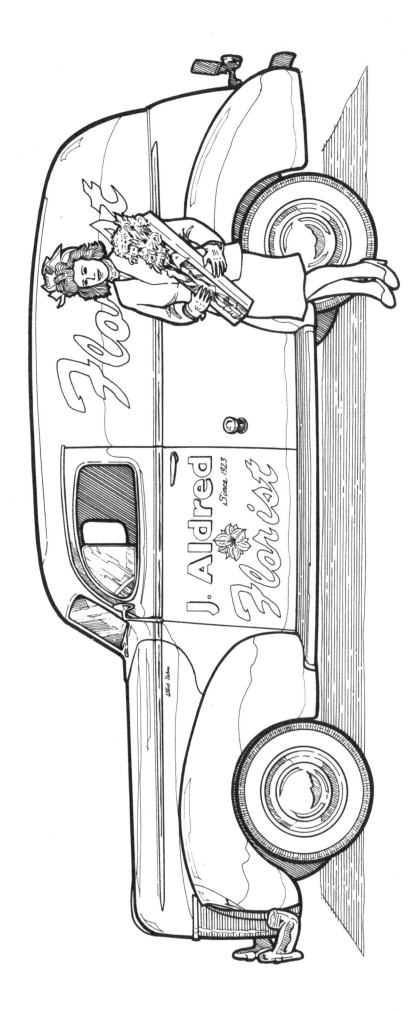

1940 Ford Deluxe Delivery Van. Considered one of the best-looking commercial vehicles ever produced, this Ford Delivery Sedan was available with either a V8, 136-cubic-inch, 65-hp engine or a V8, 221-cubic-inch, 85-hp engine.

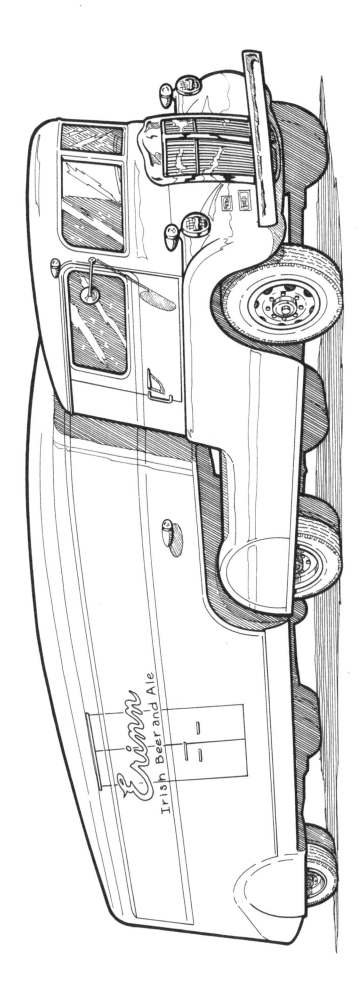

1939 White Tractor with Fruehauf Trailer. Another truck heavily influenced by the movement toward streamlining was this 1939 White/Fruehauf tractor-trailer combination. By 1921, White had become the fifth largest truck builder in the United States after Ford, Chevrolet,

Dodge and International. The company has maintained its position in the truck market to the present day, though it is now jointly operated by Volvo Motors and General Motors. Their heavy trucks are still a common sight on American highways.

1940 Reo Model 19-AS Express Delivery Truck. Reo Motors' long and illustrious history in the manufacture of trucks began in 1908 and continued until 1967. One of their most famous models was the "Speed-wagon," introduced in 1918; its name was adopted by the rock group REO Speedwagon in the 1970s.

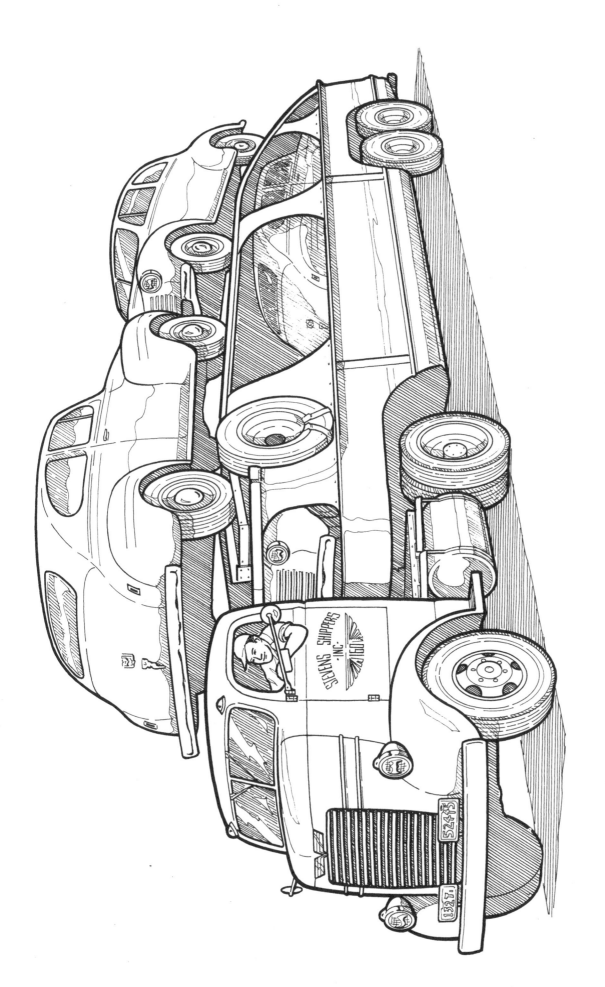

1940 Dodge Car Carrier. Chrysler Motors maintained a large share of the American truck market during the 1930s and 1940s by producing vehicles under the Dodge, DeSoto and Fargo nameplates. Dodge trucks alone accounted for more than 60,000 sales in 1940. The trucking industry became so big that by 1941 more than 4.5 million trucks were registered in the United States. The Dodge tractor shown here was equipped with a six-cylinder, 217-cubic-inch engine generating 82 hp.

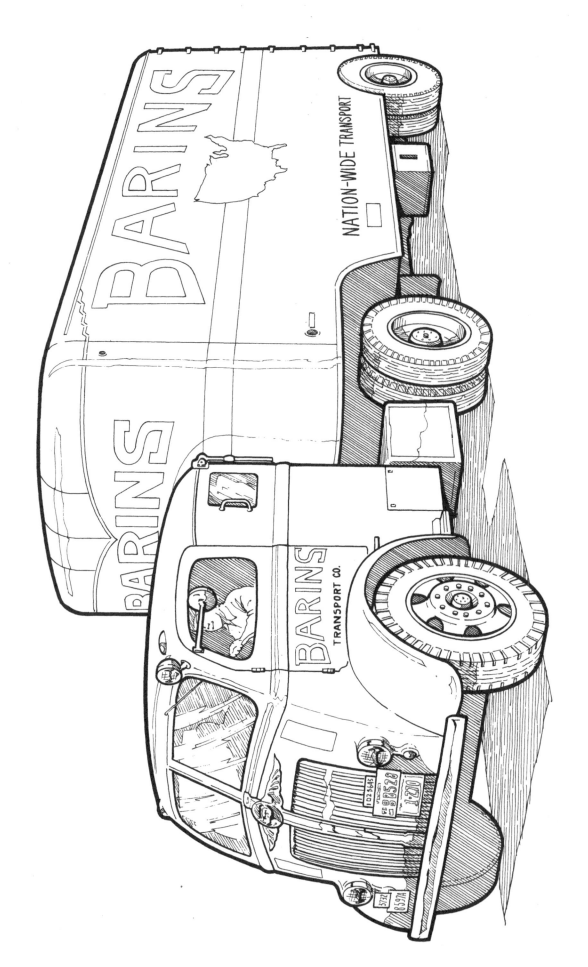

1941 White Tractor with Fruehauf Trailer. This cab-over-engine tractor featured a sleeper cab for long-distance hauling. It was powered by a six-cylinder engine developing 130 hp. The distinctive snub-nosed cab was partly the result of various government restrictions on the overall length of heavy trucks. By designing a shorter tractor, a longer trailer could be pulled, allowing for more cargo capacity. This restriction on tractor length was abolished in 1982, and since that time the cab-over-engine tractor design has been on the decline.

1941 GMC 3½-Ton Gasoline Tanker. Another stylish truck from the era of streamlining was the GMC tanker shown here. It was powered by a six-cylinder, 228-cubic-inch, 80-hp engine. The Truck Division of General Motors was about to gear up for the massive production required by the American military during World War II. From 1941 to 1945, GMC produced 854,000 trucks, 198,000 diesel engines and 38,000 tanks.

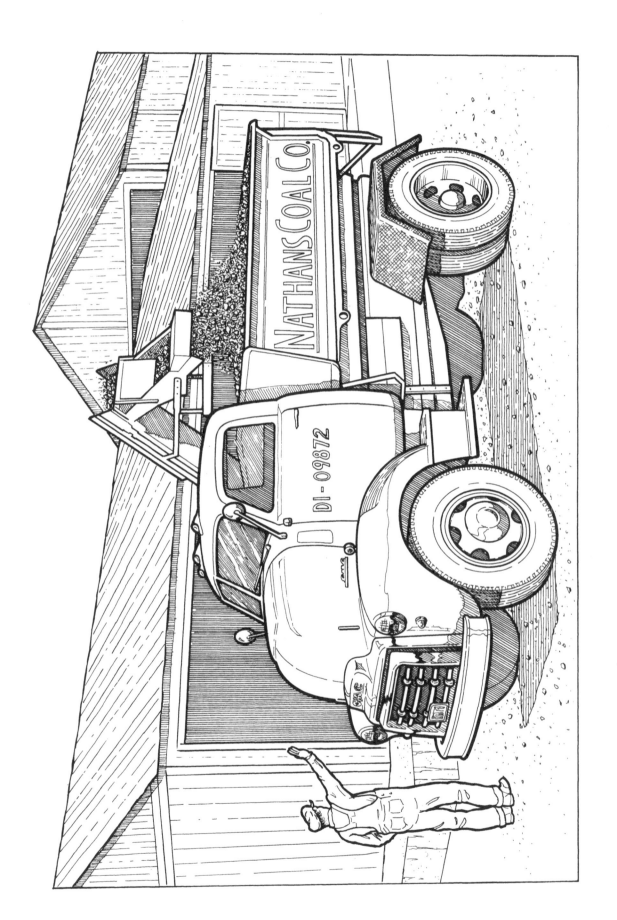

1948 GMC Coal Truck. The years immediately after World War II were boom years for American truck production. A total of 1,035,174 trucks of all types and models were built in 1948. The sales leaders for that year were Chevrolet, Ford and International, followed by Dodge, GMC and Studebaker. The coal truck shown here was powered by a six-cylinder, 228-cubic-inch gasoline engine producing 93 hp. It had a gross vehicle weight, including fuel and a full load of coal, of 16,000 pounds. At about this time, the gasoline engine was giving way to the diesel in the majority of American heavy trucks.

1951 Ford F-5 Platform Stake Truck. Ford maintained a significant portion of the light- and medium-truck market during the 1950s. Their popular F series was introduced in 1948. This F-5 platform truck came equipped with either a six-cylinder, 226-cubic-inch engine or a V8 239- cubic-inch engine. It had a gross vehicle weight of 14,000 pounds and sold for $1,895. In 1951, Ford manufactured more than 141,000 trucks of all types.

1953 Diamond T Tractor with Leach Disposal-Body Garbage Truck. The Diamond T Motors Corporation, founded in 1905 by C. A. Tilt, built automobiles until 1911 when they decided to concentrate solely on the manufacture of trucks. The company continued to build high-quality trucks well into the 1960s. The garbage truck shown here had a

Diamond T tractor and chassis with a disposal body made by the Leach
Company. The entire cab tilted forward for service access to the engine.
It was powered by a six-cylinder, 91-hp engine and had a gross vehicle
weight of 26,000 pounds. Diamond T truck production for 1953 was more
than 10,000 vehicles.

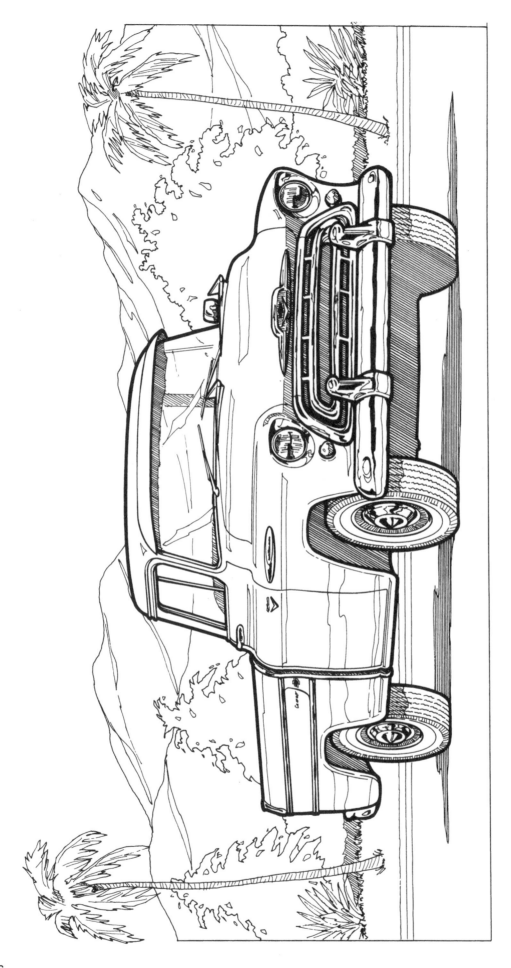

1957 Chevrolet Cameo Carrier Pickup. Chevrolet introduced the stylish "Cameo Carrier" pickup in 1955. Its design emulated the "jet age" look of many automobiles of the late 1950s and early 1960s, with lots of chrome trim and moldings and a massive chrome bumper and grill. The body panels that formed the pickup bed and the tailgate were made of fiberglass, an auto-body material that Chevrolet had experimented with in the production of its legendary Corvette. The Cameo was equipped with either a six-cylinder, 235-cubic-inch engine or a V8 engine of either 265 or 283 cubic inches. Chevrolet discontinued the Cameo in 1958 after building 10,000 vehicles. This relatively low production number makes the Cameo a rare and valuable classic prized by vintage-vehicle collectors.

1957 Studebaker Half-Ton Walk-In Delivery Truck. One of the most familiar sights on American suburban streets during the 1950s and 1960s was the ice-cream truck. With bells ringing or a recorded jingle piping from its roof-mounted speaker, it was a Pied Piper call that few children could resist. Studebaker Motors supplied many of these ice-cream trucks. This model was available with a wide range of engines, from a six-cylinder, 92-hp model to a 170-hp V8. Studebaker truck sales for 1957 totaled more than 11,000.

1959 Chevrolet El Camino Pickup and 1958 Ford Ranchero Pickup. The current popularity of pickup trucks and sport utility vehicles can be traced to the late 1950s and these two competing vehicles. The Chevy El Camino and Ford Ranchero were both based on each manufacturer's popular full-sized automobiles. A pickup truck bed was simply grafted onto the spot where the back seat and trunk were sup-

posed to be. The styling of the Ranchero was based on that of the Thunderbird sports car, and it could be equipped with a 352-cubic-inch V8 engine pumping out 300 hp. Not to be outdone, Chevy brought out the El Camino, based on the styling of the Impala sedan. Both models had lots of chrome and those big, beautiful tail fins.

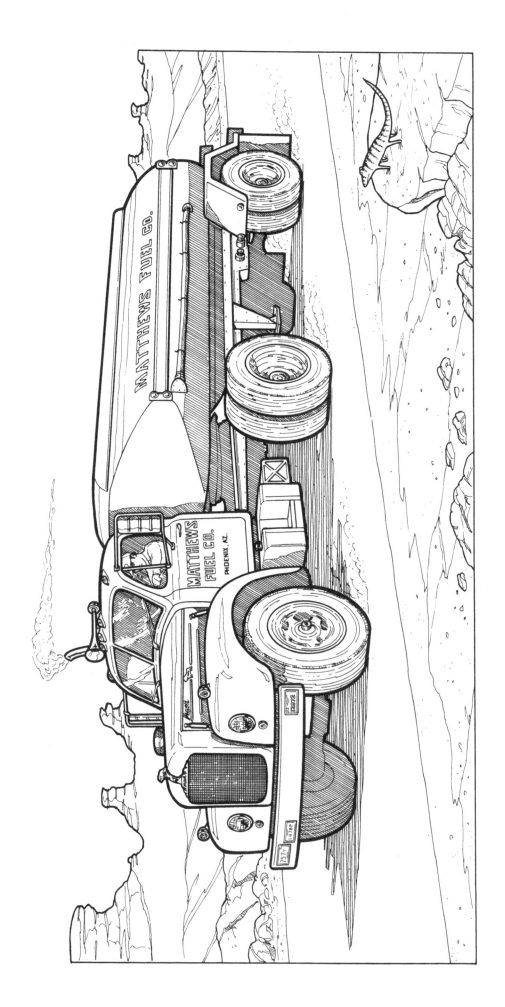

1961 Mack B-61 Tractor with Heil Tanker. This Mack tractor with a Heil tanker unit is considered a classic "big rig" of that era. Mack built more than 47,000 B-61s. They were equipped with diesel engines ranging from 250 to 375 hp. By the 1960s, heavy trucks were almost exclusively equipped with diesels, with engine builders like Cummins, GMC, Detroit Diesel and Caterpillar dominating the industry.

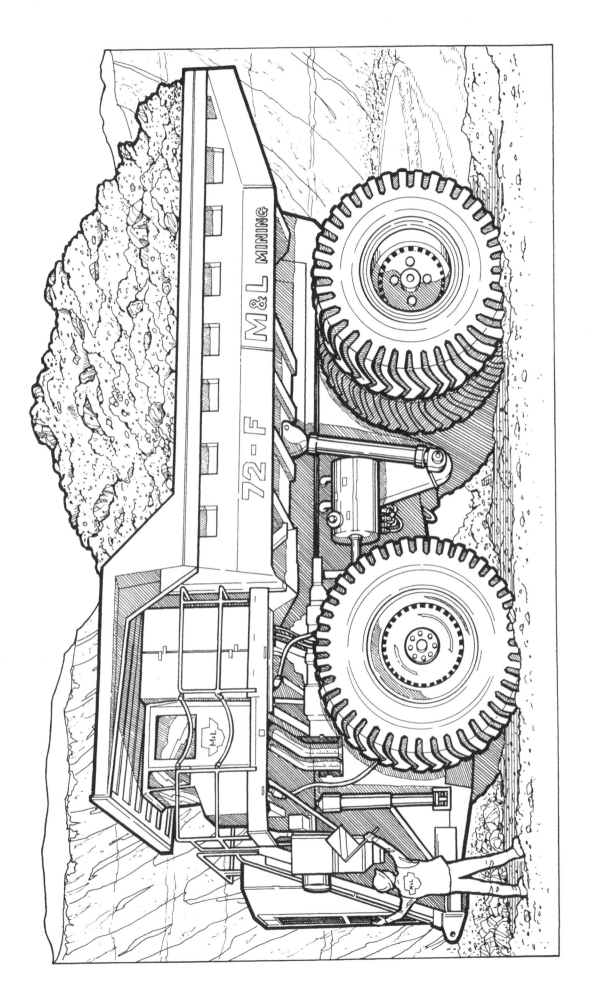

1971 GMC Titan Model 33-15C. Some trucks are designed for very special purposes. One such vehicle was this massive GMC Titan ore carrier. It was designed to carry as much as 170 tons of rock and ore around open-pit mining operations. It was 22 feet high and had 12-foot-high tires. The power for such a behemoth was supplied by a 1,600-hp diesel running an on-board electrical generator that powered electric motors at each rear wheel—the same principle as that used in a modern diesel-electric locomotive.

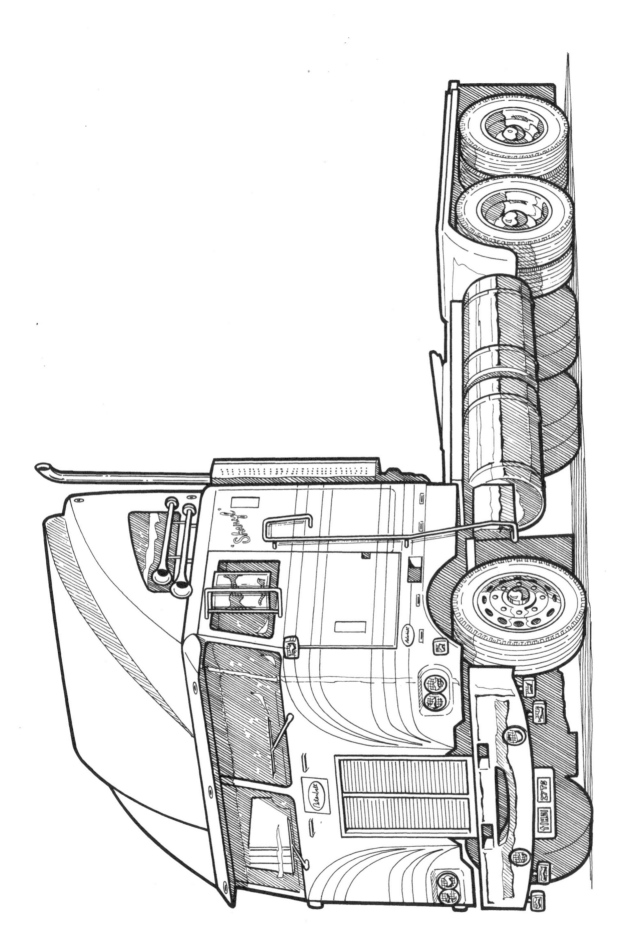

1979 Peterbilt Cab-Over-Engine "Big Rig" Tractor. Two companies, Peterbilt and Kenworth, have earned reputations for building the "Cadillac" and "Lincoln" of this class of heavy truck. This "Big Rig" was 60 feet long and weighed more than 80,000 pounds. The cab over the engine featured an aerodynamic roof fairing housing a sleeper unit.

Roof-mounted fairings of this type became popular during the 1970s and 1980s as a means of increasing fuel consumption by reducing air resistance. This model was equipped with a 425-hp Caterpillar diesel engine.

1984 Jeep CJ-7 Off-Road Vehicle. Whether they are called four-wheel-drive, off-road, or sport utility vehicles, machines like the Jeep CJ-7 have opened up new possibilities for recreational motoring. Such vehicles are given extra-heavy suspensions, oversize all-terrain tires and more powerful engines, and they are at home on dirt roads and wilderness areas. With their powerful engines and light weights, they are aptly named "mechanical mountain goats."

Monster Trucks. Since the 1970s, trucks have even come to be used in a form of motor sport involving rolling over and crushing old cars. Most monster trucks are highly modified, full-sized four-wheel-drive pickups like the Dodge Ram, Ford F-150 or Chevy pickup. The chassis and suspen-

sion are rebuilt to accommodate the mammoth tires, which can be as much as 72 inches tall. Monster-truck engines can have as much as 1,000 hp and the trucks can weigh as much as 20,000 pounds.

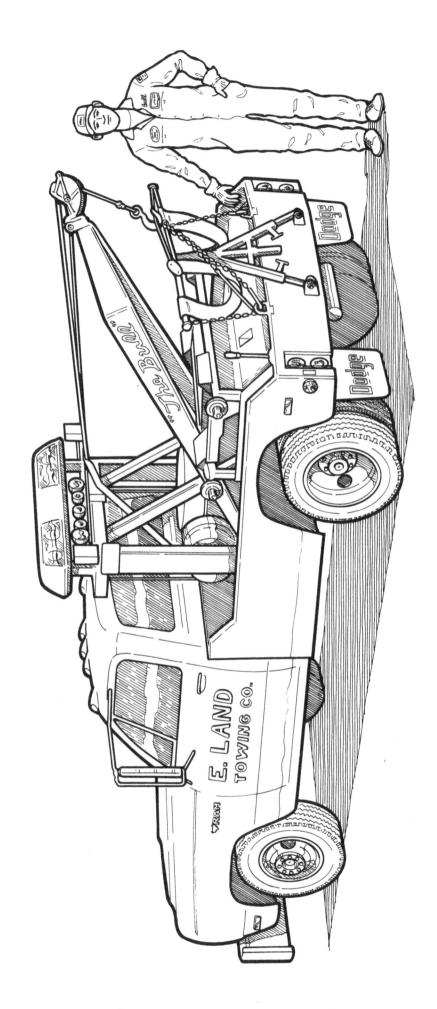

1985 Dodge Ram 528 "Retriever" Tow Truck. Sooner or later in their driving careers, most motorists will be the victim of a flat tire, a mechanical breakdown or an empty gas tank. When that happens, the flashing light of a tow truck is a welcome sight. This Dodge Ram "Retriever" was equipped with dual rear wheels and a heavy-duty suspension. It could be equipped with either the well-known 225-cubic-inch "Slant Six" 95-hp engine or a 360-cubic-inch V8 producing 195 hp.

1990 Freightliner "Long-Hood" Tractor. The "Long-Hood" tractor is an example of the modern aerodynamic look adopted by many heavy trucks. It featured a roof-mounted trailer fairing, flush headlights and fenders, and streamlined side panels covering the truck's enormous fuel tanks. It was powered by diesel engines ranging from 405 to 520 hp. Freightliner trucks have been in production since 1941 and have an excellent reputation. They were the industry sales leader in 1993 with more than 40,000 trucks sold.

1995 Ford Explorer Sport Utility Vehicle. Larger sport utility vehicles like the Chevy Blazer, Jeep Cherokee, GMC Jimmy, Ford Bronco and the Explorer shown here are usually equipped with powerful fuel-injected V6 engines and automatic transmissions. They allow motorists to explore off-road while wrapped in the comfort of leather seats in an air-conditioned cabin with high-fidelity stereo systems.